THE GATE TO GOLF

FIG. 1

" *The Gate to Golf.*"

THE GATE TO
GOLF

BY

J. DOUGLAS EDGAR

French Open Champion, 1914
Canadian Open Champion, 1919

EDGAR & Co.
St. Albans
England

CONTENTS

CONTENTS—*continued*

ILLUSTRATIONS

ILLUSTRATIONS—*continued.*

Preface.

We are born into this world, not for ourselves, but to help others."

Play Golf Well.

HAS it, I wonder, ever struck the reader how much the greatest players of the present time, amateur or professional, differ in their style and method of playing and yet seem to get there more or less consistently? They have different stances, different kinds of swing, different lengths of swing, different finishes and many have even different grips. What is their secret? Are there several ways of playing golf of the very highest order? NO! there is only one.

. Great golfers have individual peculiarities of style and method, but they have one attribute in common, and that attribute is *the* essential of good golf. Some people call it "The Pearl of Great Price," others "The Golden Key to Golf," or "The Master's Secret." I call it "*The Movement.*"

To explain what that movement is, whence it is derived, and how it may be achieved, is the object of this book and of the mechanical contrivance which I have termed "The Gate."

Golf is a Goddess.

WHAT is Golf? Wherein lies the charm of this game which decoys thousands of new converts into its camp every year?

Golf is truly a Goddess, and must be wooed accordingly, with due meekness and humility, but at the same time with boldness and determination.

I often wonder what the layman thinks, when he meets his best friend looking as if he had lost his entire fortune on the Stock Exchange, or as if his wife had eloped with the chauffeur, and, on enquiring the cause, is told with the utmost seriousness, "Oh, I was slicing my ball to-day." He was slicing his ball! Did you ever hear the like of that? Now, that golfer is not out of his mind, nor yet is he even a fool. On the contrary, he is probably a man of keen intellect, who has taken life seriously and made a fortune, and, as a matter of course, has also taken his golf seriously.

Surely this in itself is a proof that there must be more in this game than appears on the surface; that golf must be a wonderful game—a game by itself. Indeed, the effect this game has on the minds of the sanest and strongest of men is almost uncanny. No other game approaches it in this respect. Of what moment, to a golfer, is a general

election, a railway strike, or the buoyancy
or dullness of markets, when he is driving 250
yards or socketing his mashie ! Truly there
is something inexplicable about this Goddess,
whose devotees she alternately fills with
ecstacy and despair.

No game perhaps is quite so simple, but no
game surely is so difficult, so exacting, so
tantalising and so elusive.

Of what does this game consist ? Hitting a
ball ? Decidedly not ! It consists of swinging
a club in a certain well-defined manner, thus
making a certain movement with the club,
whereby in the flight of the ball the effect and
result of the swing are fully obtained.

No New Secret.

AT the beginning of this book I wish to
make one point quite clear to my readers,
which is, that I have not discovered any
wonderful new secret that has made golf easy
for myself or is going to do so for you ; what
I have discovered, however, is the underlying
secret of success of all the greatest players,
and even of the worst players when they have
unexpectedly made a good shot.

This book and Gate are not for the
champion, but for the huge majority of golfers
of the present day ; for those, that is to say,
who are not quite satisfied with their game,
who are keen on improving, as all golfers are,
but who somehow are stuck—whether at a
handicap of 5, 10 or 15 is quite immaterial—
and don't know what to do. To those I
say " Go right in and make good," for I will
assist them by means of my Gate, provided
they help themselves.

This book is to explain how to make the
best use of my Gate and to show how to
cultivate *the movement*, which, as I said before,
is the great secret of the success of all the
leading golfers. Incidentally, *the movement*
is the key I am going to give you.

I don't wish anybody any longer to say, " I
am too old, too stout, too stiff, to improve my
game." However old, stout and stiff you may
be, you can still swing the club head through
The Gate, and so obtain *the movement*, even
though you may have to widen The Gate to
start with.

Lost in a Fog.

L OOKING back over a period of some years I feel I must have been like a man lost in a thick fog, walking round and round in a circle ; or like a man looking for a secret door into an enchanted garden, many times getting near it, but never quite succeeding in finding it. In fact at one time I got so depressed and disgusted with my game that I very nearly abandoned it for farming. That I stuck to it was chiefly due to a sort of inward feeling that there must be in this game some secret or key which, once found, would put me on the right road for the desired destination. I was never lucky enough to be shown it, and it was only after continuous search that I eventually chanced upon it.

Having once found the secret I had no doubt that I was on the right road. Sometimes people have said to me, "Oh ! it is all very fine for you, Edgar, you are a natural golfer" Good Heavens ! Never was there a more *un*-natural golfer ; certainly not you, reader, even if your handicap be 18. Some time or another I must have done everything wrong that it is possible to do. I have worked on countless different ideas, but like the explorer looking for gold have had, as it were, to sink numerous shafts before eventually " striking lucky." In fact my golfing career has been most laborious, and I can safely and truly say that if I could have seen ahead, I probably would not be a golf professional at the present time.

When I first got *the movement* I at once felt it to be what I had long been looking for, and after I had thoroughly tested it in my own game and more especially with pupils who had up to then "beaten me" I knew it was "the goods"; so I set to work to devise some practical contrivance by means of which *the movement* could be most easily and most surely acquired by others.

The Gate and this book are the result.

With this book and The Gate at your command, it is then merely a question for yourself whether you become a really good player. I had blindly to grope my way up the stairs, but you have got a lift to shoot you up. And just as the movement of a lift can shoot you to the top, so will this movement of the club send you soaring in the golfing world. But remember that just as you had to get into the lift to rise, so you must also go through The Gate to get *the movement*.

"He rose the following morn a wiser and a golfing man."

My Ambition.

TO get on the right road to one's ultimate destination, does not that conjure up the secret of success in life? Surely it is better to travel in a donkey cart on the right road than whiz along in a Rolls Royce at 60 miles per hour on the wrong.

Since I discovered *the movement*, and recognised its worth, my great ambition has been to find some means of presenting and explaining it to the golfing public. It has taken me several years to hit upon a feasible method of conveying it to others in a manner both practical and simple, within the reach of every class of player, and, above all, so that each player can grasp for himself the fundamental idea of the whole thing, see for himself wherein lies its great possibilities of power and control of the ball, and feel at the same time that he can and will master this swing and so become a good golfer.

My keenest delight and pleasure in this game has not been in playing but in teaching. Often I have become tired of much playing, but never of much teaching—so many pupils with different physical powers and diverse temperaments, each with his own particular troubles to be met and overcome, have always been to me a great source of interest.

Years ago I began to wonder how it was that some players had so much difficulty in playing to a certain average standard, and I thought it must be due to fear of something, that something must be worrying them, and gradually I came to the conclusion that it was the ball that worried and beat them. I found that so long as their minds were concentrated on the swing and *the movement*, the ball did not seem to worry them at all.

This distraction proved most successful when I was with them and continually keeping their minds busy. As soon, however, as they went out by themselves their old faults returned. Why? Because the ball jumped up and dominated the situation ; because the ball, instead of *the movement*, was allowed to dominate the mind of the player. So I hit on the idea of The Gate as a distraction and mental guide for the player. I have had many disappointments in playing, but I think I may say that I have had a fair measure of success at coaching, at least my pupils have been kind enough to say so. A golf professional, however, can personally teach only a limited number of players, and as my pupils have latterly made very remarkable progress by working on this movement, I came to the decision to publish an account of it, especially as so comparatively few golfers get the real enjoyment and satisfaction that they should, owing to their playing so poorly : in fact, having seen them play, I have often wondered how some people can get any enjoyment from the game at all.

I know golf *can* be taught, and also that there are thousands of golfers at the present time who are hopelessly shackled and tied down to long handicaps, simply and solely through working on entirely wrong principles.

The Movement.

WHAT is the movement? *The movement consists of* making the club-head meet the ball in a certain manner, which will be made clear to the reader by a careful study of the photographs showing how the club-head passes through The Gate.

For a straight shot with wood off the tee or from a good lie the club-head does not travel in a straight line along the line of direction, but crosses it in a curved arc (see. fig. 17). This statement may seem rather startling to some players and quite different from the principle they have hitherto acted upon. Precisely! That is my chief reason for designing this Gate and publishing this book, as there are so many golfers at the present time who are, so to speak, groping in the dark. They may have worked hard at the game and know a certain amount about it, but while they can probably play other games, such as lawn tennis, well, they have never " got away " with golf as they feel they should. Why? Because they have bothered and worried themselves over an infinity of details without getting to the root of the matter ; they have, in fact, never got the grain sifted from the chaff.

The manner in which the club-head meets
the ball is the essential part of the golf swing.
It is in the two or three feet immediately before and after impact where the real business
takes place ; it is *there* that the master-stroke
is made and the duffer's shot marred, and it is
to this part of the swing that I am referring
when I speak of *the movement*.

It is not the position of hands, wrists,
elbows, body, etc., at the top of the swing
that makes the shot, nor is it a wonderful
follow through. It must not be concluded,
however, that the position of body and hands
at the top of the swing is of no account. On
the contrary, it is a matter of considerable
importance, for only an artist can be hopelessly wrong at the top and yet be able to
adjust himself in time. But what I do want
the reader to remember is that though the
position at the top is important, far, far more
essential is *the movement*.

However fine golf may be for the few lucky
natural golfers, I think that for those who
have acquired *the movement*—and all can
certainly do so by exercising self-control and
by practice – golf is intoxicating. It has the
exhilarating effect of champagne, without the
after-effects.

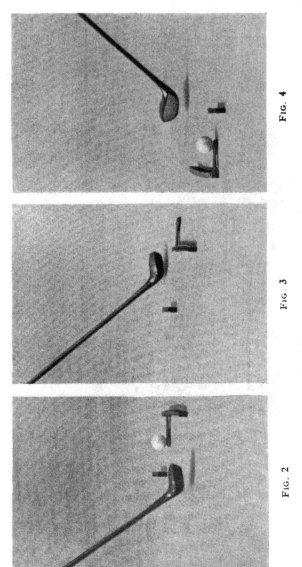

FIG. 2   FIG. 3   FIG. 4

" *The Club-head passing through The Gate," thus executing " the Movement."*

FIG. 5

The Address—" About to throw the Ball."

How to Cultivate the Movement.

THE *movement* is not a natural movement, and it will not come to the
ordinary golfer either naturally or easily;
it will have to be cultivated and practised.
While addressing the ball, the player should
have the feeling of being about *to throw*
the ball to its destination, and not to
lift it there. In his backward swing he
should get the feeling of throwing the club
round the right hip; also, he should not be
afraid of letting his body go well round also.
(See figs. 5 and 6.) This will give him a
feeling of immense power at the top, which,
if followed by *the movement*, also gives wonderful control over the ball. Many players hold
themselves in a very cramped position on the
backward swing, the idea probably being
that this adds steadiness to their game. If,
however, they were to let a little more aban-
donment and "joie de vivre" creep in, they
would drive better and farther, and at the
same time get more of the glorious exhila-
ration that this game holds in store for them.
If, then, the player has thrown his club and
body well round on the backward swing, he
is now in the easiest and most natural position to swing the club-head through The Gate,
and so get *the movement*. During the whole

of the downward swing, his mind should
be concentrated on swinging the club-head
through The Gate, thus getting *the movement*,
and for this purpose the player should have
a mental picture of the path or sweep the
club-head has to take. Just as in order to
turn a four-in-hand through a gate from off
a road it is necessary to have complete control of your team with your hands, and at the
same time to make a mental picture of the
sweep you are going to take to guide your
team safely through ; so in golf, complete
control of the club with the hands, and a
mental picture of the sweep are necessary to
guide the club-head through The Gate.

FIG. **6**

Top of Swing—" About to throw the 'Ball."

NOTE 1—Left Wrist bent but not underneath.
2—Toe of Club.
3—Body thrown well round.

FIG. 7　　　　FIG. 8　　　　FIG. 9

" The Correct Movement through The Gate."

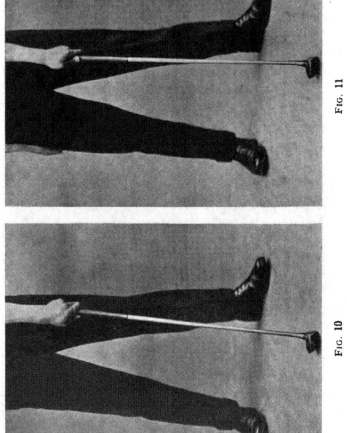

Fig. 11

Fig. 10

The Grip.

THE grip of the club is of very great importance.

I don't say there is one correct manner of gripping to the exclusion of all other methods, but I do say there are certain ways of gripping the club, whether with the left hand or the right or both, that give you a feeling of enormous power, while there are also certain other ways, by no means uncommon, of gripping with either hand which are comparatively powerless and ineffective.

A glance at figs. 10, 11, 12 and 13, will confirm this.

If the player is doubtful as to the relative efficiency of these grips, he has only to take a poker in his left hand, if a golf club is not handy, and imagine that his objective is to sweep all the vases off the mantelpiece. I fancy he will immediately appreciate the power of the grip in fig. 10. With the grip of fig. 11 he would feel equal to sweeping off all the light vases, but with the former he should feel equal to taking away with the greatest of ease the good old solid clock as well. A left-handed lawn tennis player, if he has a really good backhand drive, has practically the same grip and action as is needed for the left hand in golf.

Certain players however, owing possibly to some physical disabilities, or the approach of

" Father Time," may not be comfortable with the left hand in such a position ; in such cases the right hand should be made the master-hand. The player who is going to make his right the master-hand, should imagine trying to cut cleanly through the bottom of the stem of a thick thistle ; the right hand will surely not be placed on top as in fig. 13, but fairly well underneath as in fig. 12, so as to obtain the maximum amount of power. Nor will the club be lifted on the backward swing ; it will be slung well round the right hip in order to get the greatest momentum when it is thrown into, and through the stem of the thistle. I think there is a great similarity between vase sweeping, thistle cutting and playing golf. How very often one reads, " Which is the master-hand at Golf ? " Does it matter very much ? I hardly think so. Let the player decide for himself according to his style and peculiarities ; personally I am of the opinion that it is best for the player to use whichever hand the stroke or his mood of the moment seems to require. Some may prefer both hands to be so blending that they work as one. Golf is a more human and less mechanical game than some people imagine. To draw a ball with the left and to cut it with the right may be a useful guide to those in doubt, but after all, it all boils down to this, that whichever hand or grip seems to the player himself to be the easier, safer and more powerful to give the required movement through The Gate, must be and is for him a good grip.

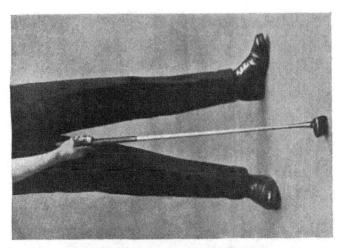

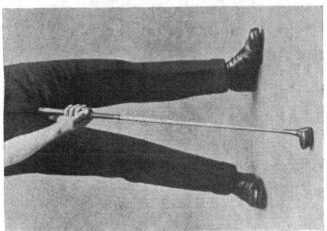

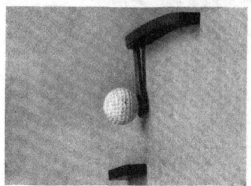

Fig. 16

Fig. 15

Fig. 14

The Swing through The Gate.

WOOD. The reader will see from the various photographs and sketches, how The Gate is set up. For the good player, the width between the points, a^1 and b^2, will be $5\frac{1}{2}$ to 6 inches. Now we come to the method of swinging through it, taking the wooden clubs first.

Fig. 17 shows the direction the club-head takes on passing through The Gate :

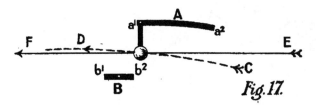

Fig.17.

A. Long arm of Gate.
B. Small arm.
C.D. Line to be taken by the club-head.
E.F. Line of direction.

The important point to note is that the line taken by the club-head is curved ; that it crosses the line of direction from left to right and continues on the outward arc for a foot or so after impact, and then turns over to complete a natural finish. This gives the swing through The Gate without touching either side. Should the sides be touched or knocked over the swing is incorrect. Take up the position most suitable, easy and comfortable, to swing through on the correct line.

Some players prefer the open, others the square stance. The latter will no doubt be the easier for the majority, because when using the open stance it is much more difficult to bring the club-head down behind to get *the movement.*

The left-handed golfer will be able to use The Gate by turning the long arm upside down.

The Slice through The Gate.

TO learn the slice The Gate is placed
pointing towards the left, as in fig.
18. Place the long arm pointing in towards
the line of direction E.F., and the small arm
parallel.

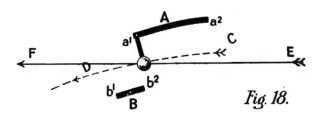

Fig. 18.

C.D. Line to be taken by the club-head.
E.F. Line of direction.

Note that the club-head at the point of impact is crossing the line of direction from
right to left. The stance is slightly behind
the ball, with the right foot rather nearer than
the left to the line of direction. The habitual
slicer will be able to swing through The Gate
in this position quite easily, and without
touching it. By gradually moving The Gate
back into the position shown in fig. 17,
and taking care to swing through without
touching the sides, the slice will disappear.

The Pull through The Gate.

THE pull being the direct opposite to the slice, The Gate is placed pointing towards the right, as in fig. 19. Place the long arm pointing away from the line of direction E.F., and the small arm parallel.

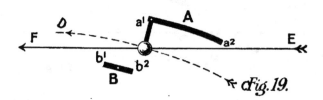

C.D.   Line to be taken by the club-head.
E.F.   Line of direction.

In this case it must be noted that the line to be taken by the club-head crosses the line of direction from left to right in a similar way to the straight drive, but at a greater angle, the stance being taken with the left foot rather nearer than the right to the line of direction E.F.

FIG. 21

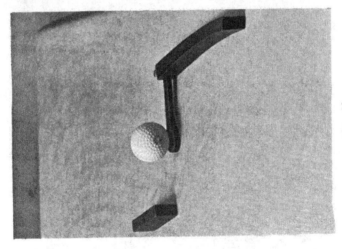

FIG. 20

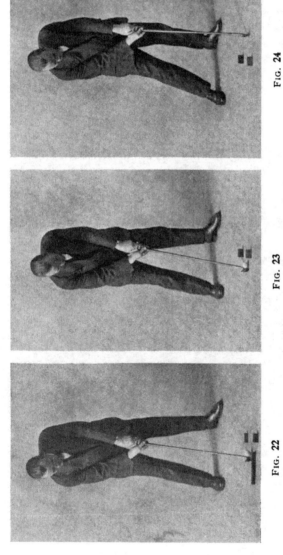

FIG. 22

The *Address*—"*Iron Shot.*"

FIG. 23

The *Address*—"*Push Shot.*"

Note different positions of head in figs. 22 and 23.

FIG. 24

Through—"*Push Shot.*"

The Swing through The Gate with Iron Clubs.

IRON. The line taken by the club-head is rather different from that of wood. Fig. 25 shows the introduction of a second short arm G, to give the player the correct movement through The Gate with iron clubs.

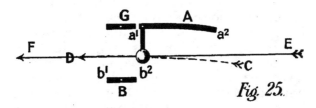

Fig. 25.

A. Long arm. B. Short arm. G. Second short arm.
C.D. Line to be taken by the club-head.
E.F. Line of direction.

The club-head, up to the point of impact, comes in on a similar arc to that of the wooden club, but continues for a short distance *straight along the line of direction*, instead of crossing the line as in wooden club play.

The player having already mastered the swing with wood, may prefer to use only the short arms B and G, which should be sufficient in this case for giving him *the movement*.

As with wooden play so with iron, the player must concentrate, and imagine swinging through "The Iron Gate" as he did through "The Wooden Gate."

Why The Movement is the Key to Golf.

WHY *the movement* is the key to Golf may seem at first sight rather difficult of explanation. Just so! Why are short stirrups the best for jockeys? Without knowing much about horse-racing and jockeyship, I imagine that when riding all " tucked-up" the rider can throw his weight forward where the horse finds it easiest to carry him. So the golfer, swinging with *the movement*, can throw his weight into his stroke in the most effective manner, in fact he can get the maximum power and control with the least exertion. Or again, just as a boxer in a certain position can get in his heaviest blow, so a golfer in a certain position can get in his most powerful swing.

Again, *the movement* consists in using the natural throwing muscles and action, instead of attempting to swing by using the lifting muscles. Fig. 6 shows a glorious position of power, for the player feels he is going to throw the ball about 250 yards, and that he has in behind the ball, all his power and weight ready to throw "from within."

Figs. 26, 27, 28 and 29 show the stance and swing when using the lifting muscles.

Watch a groom throwing a bucket of water over his trap when washing it down, or a greenkeeper with a spade scattering sand over a green.

"Every little movement has a meaning of its own."

FIG. 6

Note—" Weight and Power ready to throw from within
in behind the Ball."

FIG. 28

Attempting to go through The Gate "Lifting Action."

NOTE—Short arm will be hit.

FIG. 29

Result.—"The Gate knocked down."

FIG. **30**

Through The Gate—" The Only Way."

The Raison d'être of The Gate.

NOW I want most particularly to impress upon my readers that the whole idea of my Gate is to *make* the player concentrate on swinging the club-head through The Gate, and that answers a two-fold purpose.

1. It compels the player to concentrate his attention on swinging the club-head in a special way to get through The Gate, so that he has neither time nor inclination to think about trying to hit the ball. The Gate should be a strong and potent enough attraction to completely fill his mind, and all the cells of his brain.

2. It makes him swing the club in the correct manner which gives him *the movement.*

As he gets proficient from practice, the player will be able to narrow The Gate until he has such perfect control over his club-head that he can adjust The Gate for a pull or a slice, and still swing safely through and get the required flight with comparative ease.

"The proof of the pudding is in the eating."

The Bad Golf of the Present Day.

THE bad golf of the present day is chiefly due to the fact that golfers go out to play golf with the wrong idea in their minds, namely, to try to *hit* the ball instead of concentrating on swinging the club. This inevitably brings in its train practically all the golfing faults such as pressing, slicing, socketing, pulling, smothering, losing balance, etc. Their movement is in fact exactly the converse of *the movement*, in that in the former case the club-head is out before impact, and in after, instead of being in before and out after.

Every golfer knows how beautifully many players can swing a club at a daisy as they await their turn to start, and yet immediately they have teed up and are confronted by the ball instead of the daisy, " Phut," the swing is no more! Why? Because the ball beats them. This very unassuming little ball proves stronger than the player, who becomes physically incapable of swinging the club at the ball, as he can every time with perfect ease and grace at the daisy.

I am sure nobody will gainsay this, and yet it seems rather feeble on the player's part to allow it. Nevertheless it is desperately diffi-cult to prevent the ball from beating one at

FIG. 31

" Has the Ball a Magnetic Eye ? "

times, as I have too often found to my bitter cost in tournaments.

Has the ball a magnetic eye ?

However, once a difficulty is shown to a man half his troubles vanish ; it is the unseen, the unknown, which is so hard to overcome.

Have this out with yourself, and, once finally convinced that what I am telling you is true, you have surmounted half the obstacle.

So it is up to you not to allow the ball to intimidate and beat you, nor to allow its personality to overpower you. The ball is only an incident that lies in the way of the swing. Eliminate it, disregard it altogether if you can. " If you can—lucky man ! "

The merest tyro can hit *at* a golf ball, but it requires great self control for anybody not a natural golfer or a clubswinger to make the club do the right movement. Some golfers swing back correctly and are in an excellent position at the top of the swing to get the required movement, and then something goes amiss. Whether the ball hypnotizes them, or whether it is fear or lack of confidence that proves their undoing, it is hard sometimes to say ; but the result is hopeless. Instead of the player restraining himself to get *the movement* through The Gate, he swings blindly down, with the certain result of shot missed and, most probably, a club or The Gate broken.

The difference between a game played with a stationary ball, such as golf, and a game played with a moving ball, such as cricket, lawn tennis, or even ping-pong, is that in the former your ball is your chief opponent, while in the latter you are playing against the brains of your opponent or opponents. Golf therefore can be taught, but it seems doubtful whether the other games can be. As a rule the greatest players of the other games have either taught themselves, or more likely have had a natural aptitude or genius for them.

"Either the ball will master your swing, or your swing will master the ball."

The Fetish of Orthodox Principles.

" What is the use of worrying ?
It never was worth while,
So bang through The Gate with a jolly good swing,
And smile, smile, smile."

I URGENTLY advise those of my readers who are coming in with me through " My Gate " to forget, or at least, not to be too much concerned with certain so-called orthodox principles.

For many years certain principles of this game have been treated as sacred ; to breathe against them was heresy. Whenever any famous player has literally disregarded and flouted these principles, he has been described as the exception that proves the rule, the genius who is a law unto himself, and on no account to be copied. It seems never to have struck people that the truth was to be found much nearer home, namely, that the said principles were not only non-essential, but very misleading, once the A B C of golf is mastered.

Surely golf may be allowed to move with the times as everything else does ! Because certain principles were said to be right fifteen or twenty years ago, is that any reason why they should be slavishly adhered to to-day? Take for example that supremely orthodox and very much belaboured maxim, " Keep your head rigidly still with eyes steadfastly fixed on the ball throughout." Watch the best players; surely their heads turn a little on the backward swing. Of course, the reason why so much has been made of the question of keeping the head still, is that beginners instead of swinging and pivoting round, almost invariably have a tendency to lift the head and body on the backward swing, and so lose power; and also to lift the head to see the result before the stroke is made. The head must not be lifted during the swing, but may be allowed to turn a little, just as the hub of a wheel turns with the circumference.

Or let us consider that other equally sacred maxim, " Turn the left wrist on the backward swing until it is underneath the shaft at the top." The left wrist turns a little on the backward swing, but don't strive to get it completely underneath the shaft at top. In other words, the left wrist must turn sufficiently to allow it to be bent to a certain extent at top, see fig. 6, but, if it is completely underneath the shaft, see fig. 27, power is lost and, unless some adjustment is made later on—such as turning the club-head over after impact—slicing will result.

Let The Gate be your coach for a few weeks; The Gate is a far less exacting coach than anything or anybody else, chiefly because it asks the player to concentrate only on the one task of swinging through it, which any player can do with comparative ease, whereas it is a mental impossibility for mortal man to try to recollect one-half, or even one-third, of what he is frequently enjoined to remember to do, during that infinitesimal space of time in which the golf swing takes place. Whatever liberties of swing The Gate allows you to take, those you may safely take. The Gate only asks one thing. "Come through." Well, go through! and all other precepts will take care of themselves.

The Gate, your common sense and your brains will adjust your left wrist, will set your feet, look after your head, and put them in the most workmanlike position for the job on hand; whether it be orthodox is absolutely immaterial. After all, what is the orthodox? The Gate will not tell you to put your feet and your hands in a certain position. The Gate *will put* your hands and your feet in the most effective position.

The golfer is told his feet must be placed in a certain well-defined position for a pull or a slice. Is it the position of your feet that determines whether the ball will fly to the right or the left as the case requires? Not at all! It is the arc that the club-head takes just before and after impact, that gives the required spin whether to the right or left.

Determine then on the swing required, and then stand in the easiest and most natural position. Don't first determine how you must stand, and then hope that the position of your feet will give you the required swing ; that would be a case of putting the cart before the horse.

Find a Friend, Prove a Friend, Trust a Friend.

SOME people go through life trusting everybody they come in contact with, and, sooner or later, have a fall. Other people trust nobody, and possibly end in trusting not even themselves; their lives are one long worry, and though they may not actually have a fall, they are really in worse plight, as they are continually expecting one. The wise man, however, having once found a friend and *proved* him, trusts him.

You have found "Your Gate"—now prove him, and if he prove to you a true friend when you are in trouble and off your game, then trust him, and never afterwards forget him, even if things for the moment appear to be going well. "A friend in need is a friend indeed."

Trust The Gate implicitly, and you will play golf well.

Be happy also, and perhaps you will play very well indeed.

Practice makes Perfect.

THE majority of players will find that the best way to commence practice is to take The Gate either into the house or garden and have a thorough good chat together, and so make friends. Make a very good friend of this little Gate, and The Gate will do well by you, and tell you something that is going to make you a different kind of golfer altogether. There is no need of a woollen ball or anything of that sort; the swing is everything in golf and the ball flies according to whether the swing is good or indifferent. The swing is the essential; and the flight of the ball merely the result; if, therefore, you are an ambitious golfer, try so to master the swing that you can turn it on like a tap, whether the ball is there or not. I know that this is not an easy thing to do, but then if golf were an easy game it would not be the game it is.

My strongest advice to those who mean to improve in the shortest time possible is as follows : if indoors, place The Gate on a piece of oilcloth, and test yourself to see if you can swing through it confidently without hitting it ; then gradually narrow it, and adjust it for different flights of the ball, until you really begin to get complete control over your club. The player with control of his club and therefore of the ball, and so necessarily control of himself, is a golfer in the true sense of the word. Some may say " I could never bother " ; those who " don't bother " will never be golfers. Those who do bother will be surprised at the progress they make, and will soon find not only that they can swing the club through The Gate with perfect ease and control, but, what is more, will know and feel that if a ball were lying there it would sail away " far and true."

Now one day you will feel that you really must try a shot,—" it will out,"— so with The Gate safely tucked in your pocket you slip away to a quiet spot on the course, and put it down and try a swing through. The result is perhaps fairly satisfactory. But it seems more difficult out of doors ; perhaps the wind is a bit cold for your hands, or what is more likely the " personality " of the ball is already making itself felt. However, half-a-dozen swings restore your confidence, and now the fateful moment comes when the ball is put down. The result in all probability is a dreadful foozle. Why ? because the ball beat you. You *know* the reason, you did not swing through The Gate You smile and try again ; this time the stroke is better but not quite right ; you have still funked a little. Then you pull yourself together, consign the ball to oblivion, and make up your mind that

you will swing the club-head through The
Gate as you did when there was no ball there.
This time the ball flies away like a shot from
a catapult; and if you don't feel ten years
younger, and begin to think of challenging
some champion, I shall be very disappointed.

The next and final stage is when you have
to imagine The Gate to be on the ground in
a match. *See The Gate in your mind's eye;*
just get that happy comfortable feeling of power
and control that you had on the oilcloth at
home, then it is merely a tussle between your
will power and the personality of the ball.
Show your will power to be the stronger,
and the ball will answer so obediently to the
swing, that you will begin to think that the
great champions of the past were not super-
men after all, but merely possessed *the movement*, perfected and polished of course, by
much practice and experience.

FIG. 33

FIG. 32

Be Yourself on the Golf Course.

GOLF will never be played alike by all, no more than life is lived and food eaten by all alike. If the world were composed of people all alike, how very dull a place it would be.

The quick impulsive man will probably do everything in a quick impulsive manner, while the slow ponderous man will do everything in a slow ponderous manner.

Some days you feel strong and energetic, on others slack and lazy ; on the former let yourself go and bang lustily through The Gate, on the latter take things easily and don't try to hustle.

Nature must be obeyed.

Get hold of this movement ; school yourself to swing with *the movement* at a ball, as you do through The Gate or at a daisy ; feel quite convinced within yourself that *the movement* is "the goods," that you have got hold of it, and that it is the essential part of the swing. Then, BE YOURSELF : let your individuality, your temperament, your mind, your build, etc., develop your game naturally ; in other words, use somebody else's brains to put you on the right road—which may prevent you from getting lost, and will anyway save time— and your own personality and brains will lead you to " The Garden of your Dreams."

Finale.

AS a last word, I feel that I should like to add, " Don't be afraid to let the club-head meet the ball at a good pace, so long as you have *the movement.*" This is entirely different from going out with the fixed determination to hit the ball. Make sure first of swinging the club with *the movement,* and the more pace and nip your club has when it gets to the ball, the farther will be the flight and the better will be your golf. In fact that old bogey " pressing " may be nailed down and buried, but only provided you have *the movement.*

" The Gate will not fail you unless you fail The Gate."

To you and your Gate I wish the best of luck, and remember that Golf after all is a simple game, but never easy.

CPSIA information can be obtained
at www.ICGtesting.com
Printed in the USA
BVHW041337250719
554235BV00033B/461/P